Border Crossing

Caitlin Maling is from Western Australia. She has published poetry and non-fiction throughout Australia, the UK and the US, in places such as *Best Australian Poems*, *Prairie Schooner*, *Australian Poetry Journal*, *Australian Book Review*, *cordite*, *Westerly*, *The Australian*, *Stand* and *The Threepenny Review*, among others. She holds an MFA in poetry from the University of Houston and is a previous recipient of the Harri Jones Memorial Award and the John Marsden Poetry Prize. In 2015 she published *Conversations I've Never Had* with Fremantle Press. It was shortlisted for the Mary Gilmore Award and in the WA Premier's Book Awards. *Border Crossing* is her second collection.

For Hannah

Border Crossing

CAITLIN MALING

FREMANTLE PRESS

Contents

The Falling

I want the building
that stretches up past
the top of the white like driving

up a summer road into heat haze
that ends, might end, here
with low grey

and I never noticed the sky.
Why fear what's out of the frame?
I cannot name this city

except to say I went there once
and everywhere was white
and perpendicular and nothing

was like myself or my city.
Man has not burnt with fire,
this building shall not either.

Black has a falseness.
I grow nostalgic
for primary colours, for sound.

I think the sky is clouded
but maybe it's not. I give myself
the lassitude of stone.

I wanted none of this. Speech
beyond speechlessness.
A slow lyric.

Step away from me,
back towards the cars
parked resting in a row.

I want to gather together
our last breaths
and float.

I cast nothing behind. Step.
I'll find a piece of wood, a bridge.
I'm casting shadows you can't see.

Here. It's all the way
gone down slow.
Talk slower. We tear

tissue thin, skin,
voices the opposite
of cloud.

I've missed
the sensate elements of thought.
Your mouth

tastes metal as you fall
or as you remember
falling.

What my hand holds
is not mine
but the sensation is,

those small tendrils
of electricity.
I am never going to be a person.

I am never going to be a person
who dies in a fire,
I am never going to.

Put your face
up against
a window,

it's yours
these clouds,
slow pokes of air,

your lungs burn
even if a fire
couldn't make a match flicker,

keep this: sand, sky, stone,
the grim thing of what's outside,
your own fallow feelings,

the falling.

I-610 Inner Loop

A man wearing a sandwich board wants gold.
Another holding a piece of cardboard wants
just enough to get home for the holidays.
The light of January in Houston
makes me feel like a piece of static
in an old CRT TV.
When I'm driving I forget I'm translating
Australian English to American English,
and the birds mimicking leaves on electric wires
I mistake for forests. Houston is densely wooded
with Targets & Walmarts & Petcos & Churches & Night
Bingo & Day Bingo and none of these buildings have any windows
and in that way they are like trees.

Curving through south-east Houston,
understanding panaderia, carceria, tortilleria,
mean only bread, meat and round bread,
flattens the world out like a penny,
which is why some religions let their gods remain nameless
and from above, these concrete monoliths cup the freeways in
    their boughs,
a fleur-de-lis of faceless beauty.
But from the road if these are trees or gods
they are ringbarked ones. Neptune
banished by the towering rigs of the Gulf Coast,
trying his luck inland.

From my bed when I hear this road
I can believe it's the sound of waves.
For this I like the freeway best when it rains,
when the cars have prows and wakes. The lanes
dissolved by falling silver, cars moving only
in relation to one another.
The flooded underpasses and outer lanes
forcing us to go deeper and if it's heavy enough
all the billboards can sell is muffled light.
And after rain, wrong-facing utes
in underpasses make the descent from storm
a passage, and flowing through Galleria
in the jet stream of a road train I coast
on the memories of my stepfather driving trucks around the country.

When Mum couldn't afford a babysitter
she would send us to the docks where we would read
the truckies horoscopes over the radio,
the long cord of the CV stretched back
to where my sister and I hid under a blanket –
no children allowed at the port.
I would look at the cranes, wondering
which would be strong enough to pick us up
and deposit us in the Swan.
My stepfather told us about driving across the Nullarbor
straight through a mob of roos,
the blood and fur caught in the rims and wipers,
how when you drive you can never stop.

There are no kangaroos on the 610.
What we drive through is the afternoon,
plowing through the minutes.
In the outstretched arms of the Energy Corridor,

if I'd wanted to I could've found a love
of silt and pimple-prairie, wetlands' slowly sinking suburbs.
Even the sky isn't big, just near and heat-stained.
But summer storms find me like a Rorschach test
of where desires land, large and unmistakable. Cast out of country,
on the wind and then the wetness bedding me
in the bayou banks, asking me for roots.
Is it brave to refuse the home that's offered?
Or just another form of denying sight.
The soft opal light easing through clouds,
lifting the weeds scraggling through the pavement to our eyes.
Sun turning the tar to water, passing under the car
like pain, moving invisible beneath skin.

Closer

I take myself out
past the end of the Target-Walmart-Loews
to find the green.

Like a tourist
fumbling for language in a guidebook,
I look for home

and find translation.
Not dune but forest uprooted by a wind
long blown to brown gulf sea.

On the rustling pine-needle floor
a log slow burns, ember without fire.
From tip to tip its path is ash.

What makes a tree burn like that?
Already fallen, already dead, the other trees
just hurdles to walking.

They have no fire
unless it starts at centre, and all around
lit candles lie

making light where it can't be seen.

Tinnitus

When the cilia
of the inner ear
fail in mobility
the result
is a particular pitch,
a drone inside
the vestibulocochlear,
not loud enough
to be a scream.
You don't know it,
but that's the noise
of that tone
being heard
for the last time.
For some people,
it's silence
that brings the noise.
Their auditory cortex
alone in a room
cannot stand the quiet.

I have nostalgia
for multiple trace theory,
the idea that it's the path
the impulses take
which is the thing itself,
that the distance
between temporalities
is as simple
as any other
stochastic process.
The mind as
stock exchange.
What do we sell
for the memories
we hold?

We look to black holes
for the memories
of our universe,
in *Astrophysical Journal Letters*
a photo of shock diamonds –
galaxy-sized cosmic eruptures –
leaping out
and back in,
this gold trace on A4
what we have of that force
which can stop the stars
from forming.
We reach out only
to collapse.

Above my bed
I hang plastic stars,
they first need light
to glow.
Sometimes in the dark
I am visited
by the constellations of home,
other times I feel clearly
the path of my feet
down from Cott beach,
the hot bitumen,
the peppermint leaves
under our lips
as we try to whistle
the Violent Femmes,
our skin
blistering beneath
the sun.

First and Only Thing

I.
The men on the rooftops of Houston
never hoist a gun, only manoeuvre
shingles in and out of place, the weather
griming towards November. Still
the sinister sincerity of the hammer raised,
the man shadowed against the sun.
No harness, a trip and he falls,
a stumble and the blow is let go –
metal stunning the ground like lightning
gods release as an afterthought to mercy.

II.
It takes momentum
to hold the turf
dug up in metres
against the truck bed,
the thwack
of nail moving boards
into place. It'll hold
now, maybe through hurricanes
moving up from the gulf
or storms down for when
a snow day is more than
a flash flood over the freeways.

III.
The men on the boards,
balletic, can't fall.
Can't take the not-insured-trip
to hospital for grit in the elbow.
Can't miss the pick up
from the 11th St store,
the chance to nail things down,
nail themselves here.
It's important not to stop.
Me walking past.
The men on the beams.
The turf in the bed.
Each of us not knowing
when we'll be laid down
on the earth.

February in Oregon

Sometimes in the evening a translator walks out
and listens by the streams that wander back and forth
across borders.
William Stafford

1.
Moving between hemispheres means winter never seems to come
but just is and the sun moves with you,
reeling our steadiness toward our terrible houses.

Colours too seem the same,
the small triangle of ocean between pines
taut and pink as skin burnt by sun or by frost.

2.
From here I am level with the branches
midway up the trees on the opposite hill.

I wish to be higher.

I wish to be where it's taken
about a century to grow.

3.
There's a scrabble of life
in the brick, I don't know
how to light a fire
or what smoke does to nesting
or to imagined nesting.

4.
I must quit reading others' tragedies.
The one open on my lap about a mother
seeing her daughter through rehab. Instead –
the mist on the window is shaped exactly like Florida
and behind that trees that have never seen a hanging
hold branches over the ocean.

5.
I want to read love stories
of wherever I am. Today
I am in Oregon, the coast.
Men in rubber boots move
things in and out of the ocean.
The sun is out, despite being told
everything here would be fog, rain
and drizzle. This is a cruise ship town
out of season, closed stores
selling "generously scented candles"
and crystals. My love story
is boring compared to the idea of
two people meet. The sky turns winter,
salt-chapped lips and clutching one another.

6.
It is only 40° here by the coast,

which is warmer or cooler depending

on whether you are used to waking to frost.

7.
Somewhere people are already burning
oil for the winter. This is a great mystery to me
and it's a dying one. Cruder things
lower on the carbon chain are less used, remaining
only in those spaces which can't afford refinement.

The whales swim off the coast here,
moving blubber through the arctic, skin
unpierced and undrained, so old a species
they contain their own fossil, own fuel.

8.
I read all the bats are dying.
Fungus on their noses
like sugar on a child eating a donut.

9.
I am cataloguing sunsets.

In many ways I am suspicious
of how the light changes earlier.

No one comes to my door
but the light and the branches
knocking the boards for an answer.

10.
Answers are just echoes, they say. But
a question travels before it comes back,
and that counts.

What matters	is not mistaking rain
for feet	on the roof above you.
This leads to fear,	when it's only water
moving down	to be taken up again.

11.
It could be branches,
sparrows or the bats
I don't see now
but remember fearing
and knowing were there.

12.
Such calamity,
the pinecones falling on the tin.

My first day here
I saw a deer, a herd of elk,

now I watch the small triangle
of water between trees

and imagine waves
turning in

and coming again, *holding*
for a moment the smooth round world

in that cold instant of evening before the sun goes down.

13.
Now I know by the cold, I keep waiting for the cold to
change the colour
of the sky, make it crisper or clearer
or something other than just ice hovering over my head.

14.
The bones of last winter
in the hearth. Out the window
the Sitka spruce, skeletal
arrogant and white. The squirrel
at the last of the cones
takes an hour nibbling one down.

15.
A river runs between me and ocean
and then the head, a thin strip of sand,
the pines and shrub separating salt from the shore
hunched like a meniscus:

when a dirty river and clean river
come together the result is –
dirty river.

16.
I did not realise what I could see on two sides was water,
that what I took for clouds hung low with rain was ocean. It
is not possible for it to be truly quiet in a house; here is the
fridge switched on again cooling and now the heater drying
out the room with the same air.

17.
A building has good bones
when it keeps me warm in the winter.
The flies butt heads against the glass to get out,
seeing only the light, not the sub zero
beyond the pane.
I open only one set of blinds
framing to centre the wading gull.

18.
So cold the heat rises off my soup.
I think of the soul in children's movies,
a thin vapour only visible in times of necessity.
Here warm air meets colder air
and the moisture is drawn out, clings to my glasses
and I eat. The world is full of loss, tumbling
from the invisible to the visible,
what is left is wet and cold.

19.
I must remember that
small things/ live in chimneys/ when it is cold.

20.
I could kill them, the flies,
they are many and I am few.
The message on my phone
says be careful of elk hunters.
It would be nice if elk knew
which side of the road is legal
then they might choose.

21.
I don't know why spruce,
why hemlock, why oak or elm
or any other of the green things
using up the light.

22.
I can understand being from here
but only in early spring, when there's enough
light to walk the beach in afternoons
and enough cold to keep you from wondering
about the water. I ask a local if people swim in summer,
she says, "No they dip, it's too big a body of water."
Aren't all oceans bordered by the horizon,
sitting like an edge we are too scared
to jump off? Somewhere south
my water is warmer but no less immense.
They call it regional, this relevance –
the deepest place we have.

23.
I am under water among the weed,
tangled in what takes in light
and makes a life in the dark.

24.
Triangle of crab torso,
a mess of sunset over the water.
I am jealous of possessions.
Jealous of the sky for deciding my roof
and the colour it takes,
the line for breaking
the words from one another,

the gap of shore and sea,
the rock in the surf
dividing the breaks.
I know my boundaries
in how the breath
comes in and goes out
the skin broken,
blood indivisible as oxygen
to the eye. Knowledge circling and circling
the axons until it leaves.

25.
begin
to know the world as a land invented
by breath, its hills and plains guided
and anchored in place, by thought, by feet.

26.
I don't mind the smell
of what's fresh caught
or what's rotting on the rocks,
nor the sea lions
whose breath reaches up
off the docks to the breeze.

You say what the river speaks
of you is the truth. I plagiarise
oceans for the colours blue and green,
the difference between clouds and sun.
What song hasn't first been sung
by a wave? I am not the truth of this.
In every canyon the road ends.
Above that – storms of stone.

27.
Our whole lives have been spent
so we might end up in the sun
and the shout of sea lions
rubbing against the rocks, barking.

28.
Let the elk graze
glossy-necked and moulting –
flanks of yellow grass.
Let the trail run uphill.
Let the smell of dirt
be the same anywhere.
Let all fungi have worms
and be colour-capped
only when deadly.
The river breaks into ocean.
The ocean breaks back on the rocks
responsive to the wind. Everything we own
has brought us here.

Intimacy

During the French film,
I spend my time wondering
how I can put doors and windows into poems.

The director shoots them
always straight on, so they frame
the old man and woman in the film like pictures.

Really I'm trying not to think about ageing.
The woman in the film gets dementia,
spends her time on an electric bed.

Fewer people will ever see this film
than saw *Briana Loves Jenna,*
which is the tenth-bestselling adult DVD of all time.

In it, Briana loves Jenna,
orally, mammarily, vaginally and anally
for close to an hour.

No one enters or exits the room.
Or maybe they do
and I had left the room where we were showing it.

By that point it's hard to keep straight
the G-string, porn and cigar parties
we threw for our fifteen-year-old feminism;

hours spent deep-throating brush handles,
looking for our epiglottises in mirrors
that fogged up like windows.

The old man in the French movie
is changing his wife's diaper,
directly over his shoulder is a window,

you can't tell if she can see out of it.
In her autobiography Jenna Jameson
uses the word 'wee-wee' instead of penis,

like "he had a big 'wee-wee'" or "he took out his 'wee-wee'",
her vagina is a 'pussy', never a window,
but it often opens doors, so she says.

The man comes back from behind the door,
we see his face for a second.
I hadn't realised how I'd missed him.

I forget so many things,
we were so young, I remember.
And so tender.

At the Excalibur

He and I are meant to get married the next day.
There's a chapel in one of the turrets
or we can do as the taxi driver suggests,
just drive down Flamingo and stop anywhere.

I'm trying to think of what the dancer on the party-pit stage
is thinking but I can't. He uses the break between hands
to say, "Even you are a better dancer than that."
I know not to say to him

that the fifty-year-old waitress
bringing us drinks in a midriff top and heels,
makes me want to be outside
under a more manageable sky.

The dealers all have name tags listing their hometowns.
Really everyone says Las Vegas
but the imprecise English suggests otherwise.
Seshat the new dealer is from Egypt.

"You have a god's name," I tell her.
She would prefer I tip.
Two chairs down a woman repeats,
"Is everyone as beautiful in Egypt as you?"

I keep telling him that he looks like he's from Perth.
Which he doesn't understand. I mean
he looks like where we are from or maybe
he is where I am from.

Five double G&Ts deep I tell him,
"Excalibur was Arthur's sword."
Which he already knew.
I say, "He died for love, too."

The dancer starts to move again,
back and forth in front of us,
like how I've heard a horse does.
After you shoot her, before she knows she's dead.

California

In Monterey we walk the working-class beaches
dotted with tent tenements, the coffee hot, the motel

threadbare – neither sleep till Napa.
Then, Vegas lights and Old Vegas streets

like ghosts, like the old parts of the Colorado
beyond the canyon's rock walls, petering out into Mexico.

In the Sierra's rock pool of snow melt and river thaw
the sudden colours of rainbow trout by our feet,

our pale bodies shivering, disturb the sky
in the glass surface of the water, every nerve

awake and numbed. Mostly we keep beneath the peaks,
the middle, mostly coffee-drunk, finding our way building to building,

through suburbs, wilderness, desert, conversation that keeps
my fingers itching. No metaphors for words,

just words, the sounds of dry throats and tyres, the particular clack
of tongue hitting the bottom of your mouth. We push it,

till the car overheats and we stop, but keep talking.
We never say what we want in California.

One night I make you cry in a rum bar, at karaoke
in a private room, over ten courses of nose-to-tail

at midnight, and in the morning the Castro is fluorescent
with other fights and the harsh song of a tram picking up speed,

like a car careening through mountains after desert,
after silence and water so cold it pierces.

You always leave me even though I'm the one who goes.
Now across this country the gunmetal cliffs

and brushfires remain, the plague of cougars crawling closer
to town remains, mangy animals, still deadly, hunting alone.

The road remains. Pieces of tyre, little cracks from stones,
sunburnt window-side arms. Our country enfolded in this country,

fits more than once like lengths of rope. We drove in both.
Here I am and here you were, parallel but close. Where I imagine you

love me, in the space between eye and lid, rubber and bitumen,
here and there, frontier-crossing, the line between states,

threading the hole in the vowels that lengthen
California.

Gods of My Youth

At night we leave the colony to go to the ballet:
Balanchine, mixed repertoire, Tchaikovsky.
It's American Girl Night and the girls in pigtails and gingham
carry dolls in pigtails and gingham.
Blondes with blondes. Brunettes with brunettes.
On stage the corps dances the garlands,
such unison, such unison. While, with poise and grace,
across countries my sister slowly bleeds out
the last of what would've been a baby
and at intermission I text her.

On the stage the man lifts the woman above his head
and the girls and the dolls gasp and sigh
and I hear my country roar inside me.

It's important to have control.

You Are What This Show is All About

The young girl with the unfortunate mohawk
is being voted off the singing show.
The host with incisors like headlights hugs her,

tells her, "I remember when we first met you,
you were an ordinary girl from Kentucky with a dream."
And in the montage they cut her hair,

dress her on show days in clothes that cost more
than her mother's wheelchair and now she's crying.
She "tried to set an example for young girls everywhere

that if you never give up on your dream you can get here".
Where "here" is her mother also crying,
she "tried to give her everything but the car accident, you know",

and her mentor says, "You taught me so much,
when you sang 'My Heart Will Go On' in the semi-final,
I like *felt* that and you – *you* will go on, I know it. I mean really

really we can see you blossoming." I change the channel
to two thirteen-year-old girls huddled before a computer.
A voiceover says, "Labiaplasty

is one of the fastest growing cosmetic surgeries,
the alignment of the labia minora and majora
in a way that is aesthetically pleasing to the consumer."

The girls laugh, point at the screen, say,
"Well, if mine looked like that I'd be like so grossed out,
man, I'd have to like cut it or something."

The woman I watch television with says
she's "never even looked down there".
"I have," I say, "but I still don't know."

Back on the singing show everyone coos.
"Look how far you've come."
"Look how far you'll go."

Calf Scramble

The boy at the rodeo holds the rope
to the cow even as it kicks
his head. On the ground,
his lip split, he says, "I had to do it,
so I did it." The central monitor
shows his mom on her feet cheering
surrounded by three teenage girls (daughters?),
no man (no father?). "We need this," he says,
"I promised my mother I'd do my part."
We can't tell if he's lost a tooth
but he's upright. They are all provided
with white shirts so when they fall
(and they do) we see the dirt, the blood.
It's after the chariot races
when the horses trace ouroboros
and fling dirt over the crowd.
Ten calves loosed before one hundred teens.
What do they get, the ones who don't loop a cow?
It smells like we are underground.
Will the boy's face scar, be the first injury
that sets? These teens with the last
of prepubescent flexibility, dislocating their hip bones
like snake mouths around the calves' heads.
Earlier bullriders aimed for their eight seconds
and now the falls show on repeat.
They zoom in on the bandaged hands
double-wrapped on the rope. Their only hold.
We hear about their world-champion fathers,

beautiful mothers, the ranches in Oklahoma.
The bullfighters, whirling in tasselled skirts,
wrangle the remaining cows
like the ceremonial dance of tartars,
making it look easy in a way which seems mean
but isn't. They coax the calves towards the children,
who fling their ropes again and again.
We laugh and cheer, funnel handfuls of popcorn
buttered and salty past our teeth. No malice,
only hunger. The boy's nose drips blood as he pulls
the head and tail of his cow towards the centre
to be counted. It won't move.
Just allows its extremities to be bent in.
Then it falls. The boy still holds the rope.
After several minutes, the announcer tells us,
"Everything is all right, sometimes they just lie down.
You'll see it'll get up." Only it doesn't.
Then it does.

The Bachelor: Bluebeard's Season

It's easy to picture these women
hanging from hooks in a basement.
One says, "I have a sparkle, I won't let them
take it." Everything is production edited
down to madness, a flock of Ophelias
with side-braids. I haven't mastered
how to talk about other people
without talking about myself.
People find themselves sometime
or never, common wisdom
like Shakespeare's fatal flaw.
I'd like a lustful one, too quick
am I to pride. A returning contestant says,
"I really know who I am now
and I can be happy." Another, "I've learnt
so much about myself and I'm thankful."
At the reunion show they celebrate
having recovered from their descent
to the cellar. Their heads, retrieved,
are now screwed on right. I need reminding
that not everything is a tragedy. A better
theory of Shakespeare is one of mistaken identity.
Lady Macbeth mistakes herself a king.
Ophelia that she is loved.
My mother says there's nothing wrong with me
but melancholia and even that might be cured
if I stopped thinking I was special
and spent more time doing the dishes.

The Object

I wanted a cotton couch
so I didn't sweat
where I sat watching
the animals move in the park.
Houston water-thick
and sluggish as blood.

I never loved
the way I was supposed,
like a mosquito
drawn back and back
to the hand
swatting it away.

Comfort, yes,
like cotton swaddling,
the air conditioning,
the streetlights
keeping everything
visible from a distance.

The dogs
running back and forth
in aimless joy.

The Huntsman's Wife

I said take the children,
I said I can't anymore,
I said there's not enough wood
        for the winter.

The girl holds her brother
        to keep them warm,
in the nights they breathe together,
            I hear song.

When did the snow come?
When was winter not the time of plenty,
        you taking your chainsaw out for the neighbours?
It's how we met, you on the snowmobile
        dragging branches down the hill.

        And now?
The windows are frost and the ground is ice
and all next to the cabin is cleared.
        It never thaws enough to grow back.
First it took an hour to down an oak.
        Now you're gone for days and bring back only hemlock.

The children breathing at night
and the wind and snow and all that white
might be silent but it's loud,
        like when the wolves caught the last moose calf on the lake.
After the calf's jugular was severed
the mother just lay down.

43

It took the snow days to cover the red.
>>That was two years ago
>>when they were still drilling,
>>when they said there was enough left for all of us,
>>to just be patient, let them lay the pipe,
>>to find a way into the deep pockets.

>Just listen,
it doesn't hurt. You just lie them down. Just listen
there's nothing left alive to make a difference.
Softer than a bed. All that fresh snow.

>You just lay them down.
>Out near the pipeline.
>>Tell them to follow along it
>>Tell them if they whistle
>>it will lead them home.

Fear Letters

I.
The staff constantly working down the railings,
piles of the stripped wood blowing across the deck,
the smell of cedar absent on this cruise ship.
Too high above the water to hear the sea
pushing against the pine, the word against the grave.

Today scientists teleported one iron atom in a microchip
from one location to another
faster than the speed of light,
because quantum entanglement means
that subatomic particles in the chip – in you –
are attached in some indescribable way
to particles anywhere else in the universe,
so that if you stop one from spinning
the other must stop spinning too.

II.
Out of the water, boats are sandblasted.
My stepfather's hip bone separated, calved
and settled out near the skin. He can't fish
or turn in bed, no one knows how it occurred but it did.
We're all elsewhere, my siblings and I.
Only my mother stays tethered,
watching the swimming pool and smoking,
as if over the horizon of gum trees
and the primary school, a boat might sail into view.

I've grown my hair out since the molluscs cut my knees.
I'm full of the knowledge of that river;
what use are its tides to me inland in the north?
The difference between three and five rungs is scars.
At low tide you wait for the wake to lift you up
out of the cutting zone. At high tide
when the water tongues at the planks,
when the boats fly by dragging donuts like chariots,
you float in the brown waiting for the sun
to let you know where there's room for your head.

III.
I mistake the words seismic and erogenous often.
"It's an erogenous zone," I email about California.
Now in Alaska, I'm so tired my bones have settled
straight like a scarecrow. What faults
still run are buried. It's old, this land. Mountains pressed
onto the remains of the species from before us.
I will not know age like this,
the compression and warmth of burial among others.
Instead I sit bare like the ghost trees
from the '64 quake, only trunks left,
not fallen but branchless, pushing
where they might touch another
or be moved by a wind. Sitka spruce
and hemlock, the sag of branches, the calf
of whale and ice. What they reveal of longing
and the pang of the salmon hatchery.
The swim upstream and back. All this for pet food.

If you want soft meat,
kill a moose when it has rutted
and stroked the velum from its antlers.
This is how you survive.
As though by observing the snow fall
we might trick ourselves
into making meaning of eighteen inches this year,
silencing the whip crack of glaciers.

Truthfully I think I'm more
what the glacier grinds off the valley floor,
dirty, moving further away from sea.

IV.
Take the cellulite on the young girl's leg.
Make it something about ageing. Thirty they tell me
is about when you find yourself. Enough years
to make a picket fence from. Did I ever want a garden?
Dirt under nails is like scratching the roof of a coffin.
Are you willing to be buried? Do your thighs dimple
pressed to the plastic seat like lakes
beading on the sides of mountains?
Next to me the man leads the woman through daily Bible study,
psalms in columns like posts between here and there.
Amen, she says, turning the pages, opening them.

There was a word I wanted for this.
For what fire means in desert. For how, once a decade,
the terroir of my home catalyses a wind into a fire
that can be sustained by air alone.

Now out my window, like the red eye of Mars,
a satellite orbits, flinging at the ground
the ordinary thoughts I wait to hear.

Lot's Wife

The cruise ship had ten floors
named after sunsets.
The girls in one room.
Our two beds pushed together
making a queen.
It was our anniversary
when we sailed in sight of the glaciers,
blue and cracking.
In the theatre,
the conservationist showed slides
of the ice fields
blackened by what falls back
from the sky.
It makes them melt
faster. The boat didn't rock
as the ice calved.
Even in front
there was no push.
"Look forward," you said,
"god takes care of what's behind."
But maybe I wanted to be ash,
to fall down
from such great heights.
You only lived grudgingly.
So I walked past the aft,
saw the smoke from the engine,
everything burning to keep us pushing.
I only thought to stay still.

Salt can't be dissolved completely,
there'll always be some part of me
floating towards an aorta,
laying out on the glacier
hardening the ice for birth.

Peak

Why is it easier to believe the car will crash,
the wheel drop and piston force iron through hood,
than to imagine having this momentum forever?

I'm always being told that moving parts break,
that this is friction. It's tempting to make a corrosive
out of breath, the wind moving past us.

There is less of me today than yesterday, it's in the numbers:
miles walked over what has been taken in.
I have desires to choose the parts to be worn,

to be off these mountains on the flat of older ground.
That a body bloats in water while a stone is polished
seems unfair. Even our bones are porous as hearts.

Checkpoint

Having all the valid documentation is not enough,
nor the one hour wait, the voice over
calling us to our windows by our numbers,
the woman with two infants crying
and the man playing rhumba music loudly
through the speaker on his iPhone.

The warmth of your thighs sticking to the seat,
sweat beading behind the atlas vertebrae,
not enough to prove you are here,
part of you must be elsewhere, part of you
can't be found in the computer.

I know all my numbers by heart.
Which parts expire and when,
committed to resolving these small arithmetic,
the things that can be counted,
suspicious of devices measuring steps and breaths,
the increments of the heart flying
like Zeno's arrow at the wall.

And still I'm not here.
My picture taken disappears.
My fingerprints on the glass cannot be retrieved.
In the mirror I tell myself my dates,
entries and exits healing over, picked open.
These are the places you have been.
The last stamp – this is where you are.

Border Crossing

One.
Bayou

I.
As we enter Louisiana, Mother spots an alligator
squashed on the side of the road
and says, "I like them."
But really it's this road she likes,
high and straight
across the water.

II.
Back home, when they interned the Germans
they renamed all the towns and streets.
These are the routes we have lost.
But point to the north,
through Pitjantjatjara country,
where water appears suddenly
at the end of a road,
a breath, or a life.
Once in a generation it rains,
then the Eyre fills – the lost brought back.
From the salt and dirt, scaled hatchlings
are swift-devoured by cranes.
Where I am now is north of there.

Two.
Pontoon

We buy bathers from Walmart in fabric so thin we burn.
Mother pushes an empty cart past a flag.
"They fly that everywhere," she says, "these Americans,
they're big, drink cream in coffee, carry guns,"
and she leaves for Australia.
Later my sister and I dangle our feet in the water,
which is clear, but looks black. "Like oil," my sister says.
Then we count the lakes we have swum in at home,
Hamelin Pool, Serpentine Falls, Blackwood River.
"All of these," I say, "are estuaries." Then we try to float.
There is no buoyancy in fresh water.

Three.
East Texas

It's hot like I want to think it only is in Texas after it rains,
like someone's tipped bathwater all over the afternoon
and by the way my sister has her breasts pressed into her towel,
I can tell that Randy (two terms of service; disability pension; Baptist)
is bothering her. "Girl," he says, "I just spent $200 on my truck
and now it runs so smooth."
A man in a bar once told me the vibe I emit is either
"get the fuck away from me" or "go fucking kill yourself".
Either way I take it as a compliment
unlike the compliment Randy pays Hannah now,
as he hands her what looks like money
but is really a psalm – *god is worth more than any currency*.
She says she'll think about it and I dive in the lake,
swim to the raft in the centre, prepared to wait.

Four.
The Ozarks Sprawl

Driving north we stop to take pictures
and to say to one another, "Each of these looks like the rest."
I thought growing up that verdant was a simile for violence,
because green where I grew is the anomaly.
Somewhere nearby are the open cut mines
and all the poor people from the documentaries.
Beauty sprawls with brutality.
Blinding.

Five.
In Mississippi

I leave my sister at the Nashville bus station
both of us not done with our road.
"You grow into it," I say, "our genetic predisposition
for anticipating loss."
In back-backwoods Mississippi,
I watch the sky pass through its stages of blue
until the clouds are flocks.
Someone has started a bonfire in a field.
At first I'm sure all I see are embers
then, among the bruised limbs
of what was Chickasaw homelands,
I see fireflies for the first time
sputtering into flame.

Six.
The Trace

It confuses me,
not knowing what's sacred.
In the grove just off the Natchez Parkway
a man sits in his Hyundai.
Windows up, engine on, phone pressed to ear.
I walk around his car
to get down to the Sunken Trace.
It isn't long; at the deepest point the path dips,
hunkers between two oaks.
Soil worn down by thousands of years and steps.
Ten miles down the road I stop again
at the bulk of the Chickasaw Emerald Mound.
The Parks Service has posted a sign *Please Climb*.
The mound was not just for burial of dead.
The living had a separate hillock for a temple.
Once I've ascended, this other mound greets me.
On top, a family poses for a photograph,
the father hoists the youngest overhead like an offering.
"Soon," he says, "you'll be too old for this."

Seven.
Ghosts

Driving home from Tennessee to Texas
I stop in Natchez, Mississippi.
In my mouth these states are marbles
(says the barman in Nashville, "You're losing your accent.")
Where I get lost are the one-way roads in the cemetery.
I'm told people come to visit a marble angel
who orients by the moon. But it's too hot for angels
among the lost soldiers of the Southern Confederacy,
Unknown but polished daily.
Before I leave town, I tour Longwood Plantation – octagonal
but never finished – its crops burnt by soldiers retreating.
A hole runs centrally from floors one to six
to take hot air up. I imagine it's like the hole of a desert oak
after its been chopped down and dug out,
only I've never seen such a thing.

Eight.
LA Border

At home, we hide our massacres
in language: skirmishes,
by-products, unintended
consequences. Here,
I keep to throughways, byways,
farm-to-markets. Every town
is too poor for a Walmart,
which must reconcile its costs
with its demands. This is the wayside
of America. "Reconstruction,"
says the man in the coffee store,
"killed the South." Now the weeds
of commerce stretch inland,
each car yard has a sale
where the repossessed are exorcised.
Only churches seem to bloom
(he died for you
and what have you done for him lately),
foetuses reclining on billboards.
Pity is just a sidestep
from disgust.

Nine.
Houston City Limits

My marriage is like the ring-roads
guarding the outer limits of the city,
or a dartboard I can never hit the centre of.
When I orienteer I don't use a compass,
I'm lost by the last marker. Shackles
are circular but so is fruit
and the moon. Roads can be binding
or they can be a loom but there's little
tapestry in the outer limits
of the eastern corners of Houston.
Just trucks, broke down and angry,
tyres spilled and thrown to the side.
Houston is a story which repeats itself:
Target, Walmart, Loews, Sears.
Ease into familiarity like a bath.
You're going home.

Sad Teen Cancer Movie

In the movie, she's dying. Slow breaths, fluid
in the lungs. He says she says
she doesn't see herself. She's beautiful.

> To get here we drive thirty miles up I-25,
> Santa Fe to Espanola through the pueblos,
> night frosting the high desert in marzipan.

In the movie they are in love. But don't say love. Instead
say you're goofy. I miss you. Come back.
Text bleeding across the screen.

> In today's *Albuquerque Journal*, peaceful protests. The death
> of a young man to police bullets. Now they say
> it may have been deliberate. The boy
> calling fire down upon himself.

In the movie, they travel to Amsterdam. First kiss in Anne Frank House
People cheer. An excerpt of the diary is heard. Back to the hotel.
Takes off her shirt. Fade to black.   How did we get here?

> The boy who actually died in New Mexico
> is like the other boys who die in New Mexico.
> Stories webbing together like film looping.

I sit where he sat. This cinema by the highway –
DreamCatcher 10 – caught by the same dreams
as in the casinos that reach up and down the interstate.

The movie boy dies. There are two funerals.
He hears their speeches. First when he is alive.
Then when he is dead. We know he is dead
because they rehearsed us for it.

Over each funeral we see his life. His love. It's sadder
every time. This is how we know it's not real life.

The girl goes to the backyard. To look at the stars.

From the freeway out front the cinema
there are no other planets. Only stoplights,
the police red and blue, broken tail-lights.
The incongruous form of a man
on a bicycle. His one light flashes
as he wobbles on the verge, waiting to fall
when there's no one left to see. Sky bright
with the stars we forgot to name.

Greenville

lucinda on the radio.
you ain't my man
& this ain't my country
my blues
the guitar in e
sorrow on the pickin' fingers
cracked against the wood.

i'd never pretend my body
was an instrument
that my guts stretched
& dried on a rack
might make a sound
rotten & echoing as a cat
longing at your door.

Aclima

Aclima never gets to murder anyone,
never gets a stone to hold.
I wish she ate her brother in the womb
or even just his name, so we hear "Aclima
and her seven daughters", "the mark of Aclima",
and before that the voice – *let's go out into the field.*
If Cain slew Abel for Aclima,
then forced son after son into her,
I would like to hear her voice raised once – *let's go –*
for her to have the name that means breath,
her, the woman who would've held the rock
warmed by the sun, its side pocked like the skin of an orange.
Ripe. *Let's go out into the field, brother.*

Organ Mountains

I saw lightning strike a plane once
and thought it's designed to take it, expects it,
how it always rains the first week of July in Cruces
where I almost step on a snake dragging a lizard
off the path, watching the black roll in,
debating whether to turn higher up the stone
or risk the lower of the arroyos.

Earlier this week a sad man told me
about an electroshock experiment on rats.
The ones that knew the shock was coming went crazy.
The ones shocked in ignorance survived.

I am not a rat. Storm flowing.
Mountains around me like a hyperbaric chamber,
the lightning staying mostly in the clouds,
I retreat to my car to sit not touching any metal,
dreading the sound it will make when, if, it hits.

Virginia Sonnet

I will not write the Penelope poem.
I will not write of weaving, of wifehood,
of the boredom that comes when your job is just to sit
waiting to be desired in the right way. The moon,
yes, is slung past the mountains in a curve,
night making me a cloak of moths if I stand
under the light too long.
Each inch of my back has wings.

Who is to say I am not the god's one?
Who is to say I am not become
a flame? That with these wings I might leap,
light up each tree, turn the ridged pines to candles
flickering. I offer up nothing. I keep my name
and this fire I bring just to burn.

Herakles

I.

I'm thinking about the man
who drove his sons into the dam.
All three boys drowned. It may have been accidental.
But the outcome is known. It's sure
he clung to the bodies,
no heavier or sodden than clouds.
That it was dark. That the road
still runs by the muddy water,
that the trees still reflect
and on clear days, the sky: a mirror.

II.

To be undone by the one you love,
you have to let someone else's mouth move yours,
open you up and drink air
down one throat.

Water is most powerful in a small space.

Why not stop and pull back? Why not wait?

Why not stay content to drive separate cars to separate places,
to eat together four nights and divide the dishes
evenly and without argument.

But her fingers, you see them down to the ivory,
see them as melody,
individual songbirds.

III.

Herakles's name contains his sins. Hera
(scorned) in *Hercules* the TV show
appears above the horizon. She is older,
beautiful, all goddess. Zeus – cantankerous
and lovable father. Hercules always at battle,
clad in a loincloth with straw-coloured hair.
My friend says, "Your dad looks like him."
Each episode a new beast, it's safe,
he never completes the challenges.
The years after my parents divorce
pass in forty minute increments,
with breaks for us to feed and water ourselves.
Hercules, ever the warrior, never the homebody,
never in the small house with the wife
who only wants to keep him warm.

IV.

Can grief come before the action?
Might he have lifted his hand to his face
and that's what drove the car off the camber?

Theories of time proliferate.
Not just the when of the surfacing, how long he dove,

but how to say who we are in the when
of the universe. Only since time
have we been able to measure our own smallness,
to know the relativity of where we are.

V.

I imagine my own father one Christmas
taking his hand off the wheel on the beach road,
his mouth so wide I didn't know
how he'd fit all himself back in.

Something only I remember.
All survived.
The car ran straight.
Each of us chose our dimensions.

VI.

The wife at first says, "No, not the man I know, no
not our sons." But there's betrayal. Another man.
She is not driven mad by grief
but the question remains:
what to do different and when? Which branch
must be cut to stop her horror from blooming?
Gravity pulls us all along our pathways.

VII.

In my heart I don't trust Herakles didn't know.
Fingers calloused but still tender enough
to feel the weave was off, his wife
handing him the cloak in a last familial act.

He'd retired from war and learnt
what brings pleasure. It's easier to love through violence
and quieter. The distance not so great
between stitching and unstitching.

You can't fight the everyday. The slow battles
of sunrises, each inch his children grew.
Time too much and not enough, pressing in
and out of him.

Does love always have to be allowing the planets
to move you as they will?

VIII.

They say cheating is hereditary,
divorce runs in families. Violence too,
is broken down to RNA, DNA, small
injuries, even just the birth canal
contracting too suddenly. All that cranial
softness it takes time to harden. The invisible
dents we cause one another
through loving, not loving, neglect.

IX.

I think Hera would've grieved to achieve this.
Herakles imprisoned, the children gone.
What would she do now? Missing the small ones
running among the fields ignorant of themselves
as descended from the stars, the pieces of air
and carbon we pump with abandon around our body.

Some things are worse than their mythic origins.
By the highway galahs sit on the electrical wires
and cry. I stay alive. It has its beauty.
The whole thing about being from somewhere
is scars, the rough places
no cell division can multiply over.

X.

I fly over Perth,
headed out over our rivers, our oceans.
I watch *Bridezillas*,
the women rip their dresses
and claw at their skin
for the idea of a family.

I want to believe we are born
nothing, that we come into being
through multiplication and division,
that mitosis is amoral,
just this stardust falling apart inside of us,
the violence in my fingers only a day or weave away.

Shreveport

The way out of loneliness
does not come from driving four hours
and trying to imagine beauty
in how the dead bushes are overgrown
with some other, less fragile, life.
The bird hops in and out of shadows
to get at the leaking faucet
and under it all the highway throbs
like an atherosclerotic aorta,
taking us where we need to be, slowly.
Life is a shell game of fleshy parts
and this emptiness, an almost dryness
perfect for burning and I never thought
I'd be nostalgic for destruction,
the catastrophic fire warning of midsummer,
the scent of the eucalypt oil aiding the burn
like a balm down the throat.
Rose bushes, even thousands of them,
even this, the biggest rose garden in the South,
are scentless when dead.
Just constellations of thorns ready for crowning
and despite this longing
I am no martyr. A eucalypt survives from a single
buried tuber, splits its own burnt bark to regrow.
One left in a field of grass
waits over a century to seed and then
life. Just a little grey finger,
already scarred, digging itself out of the ground.

Conversion

I watch people gain weight.
Not in the way a man on the internet pays a woman in another state
    to eat red velvet cake over a webcam does.
But in the way of tides and sandbanks, or tulips emerging catching
    flesh colours.
For a while I ate cake every day for breakfast. For another while,
    ice-cream.
Now, every Easter, this is the way I break open the morning. Sweetly.

As girls we had competitions to see whose thighs had the widest gap
    between them,
wider than an egg but which: chicken, duck, Easter?
As they grow now, I feel more a part of the world.
I am taking parts of it. I am turning them into myself.

***

I have an image of the world as a closed system.
A ball on the end of string, attached to other balls, with a papier-
    mâché sun at centre.
Finite parts.
The more of the world I take in, the more of the world I am.

***

Actually there are no physical boundaries.
The gravitational pull of the earth keeps atoms at different levels of
    the atmosphere.

We are kept by the gravitational pull of the sun because it is
    larger than us.
By being more I can bring things closer to me.

***

People are repelled by a certain level of weight.
Maybe weight is not gravitational but magnetic – a certain mass in a
    certain place and
the polarity shifts from attraction to repulsion.
I make a good plain woman. Plump, easy to find a footing on.
Which I like. In metaphor it still makes me a landmass.

***

Whatever the size of my tide-affected body, I am attached to all of it.
There is a follicle on my nose tip that grows a single hair to the size of a
    centimetre.
If the light catches it my husband will pluck it out.
I keep my face in shadows.
I want to see how long it can grow, how long I can grow.
Our cells are impermanent.
We remake them.
I have to take in as many as I take out.
Do the cells we have since birth say more about us than those we
    replace?

***

Several of my friends who are Catholic have 'body issues'.
One of them traces this to original sin.
Here the body is originary and originating.
There is sin and there is sinning. The body does both.

My body is created in an image.
Not from dust,
not from ribs,
unless it is in a taste for my mother's oven-baked Chinese sticky
    pork ribs.

Sometimes I look for the god inside of me.

***

Travelling through Malaysia I learn about Batu Caves. About
Thaipusam. The kavadi bearers pierce themselves with offerings.
Other Hindus pierce and hang themselves from hooks.
They pull gods from their bodies. Maybe just a knowledge of gods.

My friend in Perth attends bondage parties. At one they take up a
collection to fly down a hook specialist from the States.
She hangs herself from her nipples for the duration of a party.

***

There is a place in the brain that when pushed creates a god in
    some people and a
shining light (and the knowledge of the shining light) in others.
I like binaries.
My body/Not my body.
For a while I thought psychoses could be divided in the same way.
Into those where the person believes something is inside them trying
to get out and those where something is trying to get in.

Some people think there is plastic under their skin.
They pick it out.

Others feel bugs on their skin. They crush them in sleep. Find
    carapaces in the grit of their body.
Both types collect the pieces in matchboxes and empty pill bottles.
They take them to their doctor to say I wasn't making it up.
Almost always they are pieces of their own skin.

***

I know how I will die. I saw it in a movie.
There was a woman who was happily married.
She lived in a house she didn't have to clean. Which was good because
    she gets allergic to cleaning products.
Then to fabrics. Food preservatives.
She gets tested by pricking her back with hollowed needles tipped
    with different solutions.
The pinpricks come up like scales.
She moves to the desert.
To a cult. Or just a healing organisation.
She is allergic to electromagnetic waves. All that energy.
She moves into a plastic bubble house.
She dies.
Throughout no doctor can find anything wrong with her body.
There was just a fracture, a disjunct between her body and its being
    in the world.

If I become my body completely, become a body, a mass, I will be
separate.
Apart. Not a part.
In the best version of my death, I push off without leaving.

First Blood Part Two

Meanwhile Rambo is sad,
running through the jungle of Vietnam
that first broke his heart. Even after
he catches the snake by the head
and stares it down, Rambo is sad.
Rambo has no home and everywhere he goes
people die. In Vietnam I have only been happy.
Spending my honeymoon in Cat Tien National Park.
On the second day I realised you hear no birds there
and the trees, though dense, are young.
Our guide says, "Agent Orange." The animals
that survived were hunted all the years of famine.
On Rambo's boat ride upriver he says,
"There's a war against soldiers returning,"
that's his problem. Rambo wants to win, to survive:
"To survive a war, you have to become a war."
This is not what makes Rambo sad.
Over his head a flock of geese screech
like a knife being sharpened. Everyone asks
Rambo about orders, Rambo says, "No orders,"
and takes his crossbow. The jungle
makes jungle noises, thousands of frogs.
Rambo doesn't know why Rambo is sad.
A war shouldn't be sad. He has his knife
to trust and it cuts through everything.
The jungle. The tired frog sounds. The soundstage.
Rambo slashing out into the world like a dervish
of feelings and upper body strength. The world

has no explosions but just as much death.
Rambo wants what everyone else wants.
"To be loved just as much" as he loves.
His heart pumping like Atlas's hairy bicep
holding up the globe. None of this will bring back
the frogs, the ducks, the mangroves, or the fish.

Background Extinction

It's going to snow in the valley tonight.
We are clamming on the beach.
You find a small hole and dig.

Gloves can't keep the sand out
nor the water pooling up
and collapsing the walls in.

A slow drizzle
in a strong wind
whipping exposed skin.

It's only touch. Waiting to hit
something hard and then the scrabble
to hook it before it sinks itself lower.

Such a small amount of flesh,
fingernail-sized, pink,
translucent and salty.

Everyone says there is less now.
Or that it's not here, but there –
the other bank, tide-covered;

that there it takes only one hole
or that it used to need just a rake,
a series of clunks indicating life.

In an impact winter
no marine ecosystem survives.
We move down the beach

digging life out by hand.
How slow the universe moves
measured against our one life.

In stillness the world is a child.
Things slip by the window,
clouds and leaves, the ocean hovers

out of sight. These are simple.
The earth expands. The core will show
we were here for a second.

Desert Meditation

I.
In the Chihuahua what's human is what you bring.
Only solar power, water trucked in, propane tanks for heat and food.
The sun has burnt for nearly five billion years, fallen here for four
    million.
It's easy to believe the light will outlast us,
glints of metal sands glowing at midday. At night,
the moon is another stone overturned in the canyon,
the ground cools and the animals you don't see by day
leave the footprints you find in the morning –
javelinas and coyotes – the difference between ungulate hoof and
    mammal paw
held by the sand until dusk, when the wind blows
from over the border, over the Rio Grande,
and you don't see anything anymore. Only sand,
the rough phonemes of what's beyond the Guadalupe's
flooding the plains.

II.
Speech is unnecessary to song. The vermilion flycatchers rise
from the sotol to migrate south. The sky is the desert
we haven't figured out how to colonise yet.
What use is a border to the desert? How to separate
one grain of sand in a dry riverbed from the next?
The heat rises off the rock face, edges of stone and sky blur
pink, orange, yellow, until all work down to ink.

A stone can skip in two the river
that runs through the Boccaccillo's Canyon.
But when it floods, the plains fill and the border widens
so the tops of the yucca are the only flags,
green and greener the only nations.

III.
From the plane, flying to Alice,
the difference between the Great Sandy and Little Sandy
deserts
cannot be quantified in sand,
it's in how the shrub unfurls in widening circles,
an unfolding of vegetation.
At the top of Kings Canyon you imagine
a line between WA and the Rock.
On the surface high above the desert
the fossilised remains of strombolites
indicate this once was an ocean. In the stone,
the patterns of a sea hold.

Land does not age like people. It gets smoother.
it does not rust in water, it polishes.
Land outlasts what we call it.

Desire

I'd like a cape, a cloak,
a set of camos in time for elk season.

It's all about being caught – that
and extremities. The fingertips and toes

are the first to go. I am bipedal
in longing, the metatarsals twitch

independently. I remain upright
to hold you. Tensing my thorax

like a honeybee to warm your name.

Chacoan Stairway

I admire the person
who said not around
but up. These eight-hundred-year-old
grooves for foot and trade.

Is this how I got lost?
A child walking the bush
only in straight lines
ignoring the tracks.

I never mastered the curve.
Nor thought I needed to
but now these dirt roads
rut and cannot be trusted not to slide.

And the Chacoans?
Nobody knows why they left,
maybe heading north,
the Spanish coming from the south

and this is Navajo land now,
who say time is a circle
that travels in straight lines.

Snow Day

Texas makes me want to forgive
the girl, younger than me,
who after I say I'm an atheist,
spends ten minutes on my doorstep
asking, "What if you're wrong
and you stand before the living god?"

There are things I can't explain.
And there are things I can:
the clouds gathered in the sky,
why moisture sticks close to ground,
the oaks spreading their roots in drought
to eat this shallow rain.

Every single one of us is thirsty,
wakes in the night to drink.
It's nice to love this way,
nicer to believe ourselves loved.
But I love best that which can't
love me back.

After my first hard frost
the bushes out front turned dune green,
after the second – to chaff. It's beautiful
to watch the desiccated in the wind.
I knew and didn't know
ice could do that.

Test Footage

The trees
hit with grains of white
bend suddenly to the left
then snap back up
denuded,
slightly crooked
like coastal mallee
bent in by an easterly.
In black and white
the images superimposed
colours flipped,
the house blows apart
like sand or light,
a storm, rain
at three am on tin.

The old ways
are simpler.
On the ear, the eye,
still we fear. Now each year
the pixels grow closer,
more numerous. Saturated
colour running
deeper like all the greens
a desert suddenly displays
in the high-altitude light
after rain, so dry
easily flooded,
easily drowned.

On desert's edge,
White Sands,
then Alamogordo,
once split
piece from piece.
Restitched,
it sits invisible
from the graben
where the Very Large Array
measures what we can't yet control,
cradling light and sound
like angled conch shells
or the pearled
underside curve
of an oyster
just shucked.

Islands

I.   A nissologist is someone who studies an island on *its own terms*. What are the terms of an island?

II.   Australia is often called an island continent, sometimes *the only island continent*. Its terms are of being an island.

III.   If Australia is an island continent, then so is Antarctica. Australia is changed to the only *inhabited* island continent.

IV.   Gondwanaland is an ancient super landmass. Australia and Antarctica were the last two places of Gondwana to separate.

V.   When I was young I thought islands floated on the surface of the ocean like glaciers and that Antarctica was an island made of ice.

VI.   A few years later I grew concerned about islands floating away from one another, of Australia losing its place, I decided there must be a thin rope of land tethering Australia to the sea floor. An anchor.

VII.   Often we speak of ourselves as being *anchored* to a particular place. A *home*. Anchors and roots become indistinguishable.

VIII.   I read in a book: "*Down Home* is a psychological geography."

IX.   From Houston I always refer to Australia as *down* or *below*.

X.   Sometimes I picture myself standing, sending roots right through to where I imagine Australia is. In this image Australia becomes the sea floor.

XI.   When we look at the moon, we always say we look "up at the moon". There are no directions in space. So really we just look at the moon, and it happens that we tilt our head.

XII.   In the same book: moons bind all islands in two ways.

XIII.   Often from an island the moon is the only other landmass visible. The moon also sets the tides. Tides form the littoral boundaries and edges of islands.

XIV.   I have most often looked for the moon from the beaches around Perth. These beaches are collectively known as *the coastal plain*.

XV.   Australians are known as *plain-speaking* people.

XVI.   The best way of interpreting these two statements: Australians speak the language of the coast.

XVII.   I have no terms to explain what I see off the coast nearest Houston. From Kemah I can see land opposite me. It's possible this land is an island. It's impossible this island is Rottnest.

XVIII.   Collectively, we have no terms for what came before the big bang. If time emerged in

the big bang you can't use the words *before*
and *after* to describe the imminence of the
Universe. It just *is*.

XIX.   My husband tells me to picture a piece of paper.
To draw a circle on it. That's our universe. Then
another circle. A hypothetical other universe.
He says none of our laws apply outside our
circle.

XX.   I say they look like islands.

XXI.   He also describes parallel dimensions using
pieces of paper. He lays one on top of another.
They touch, almost occupy the same space but
aren't connected in any way we are capable of
seeing.

XXII.   This is like the squirrel I saw squashed flat on
the road in Houston. There was no way for it to
actually become the cement.

XXIII.   We don't have squirrels in Australia.

XXIV.   Deep down I know I can't touch Australia from
Houston.

XXV.   All the words I know for winds come from
the coastal plain. Easterly, westerly, northerly,
southerly. All our terms are directions for
things coming to or leaving the island.

XXVI.   On the coastal plain we tell time these by
winds. The *sea breeze* means it's the afternoon.

XXVII.   When there is a wind in Houston I look for the
coast that *isn't*.

XXVIII.   One of the terms of our Universe is that light travels at 299 792 458 m/s.

XXIX.   The sun sets directly over the ocean on the coastal plain approximately 43 200 seconds before it fades over land in Houston.

XXX.   In a total vacuum, particles will randomly pop in and out of being. This means that there can never be such a thing as a total vacuum.

XXXI.   Similarly, in our universe even if there is emptiness, there is always time.

XXXII.   In her kitchen my mother has an eggtimer which measures minutes in grains of sand.

XXXIII.   I haven't been *down* to the coast in 20 563 257 seconds and counting.

XXXIV.   There is no term for how many grains of sand I won't have touched.

Once you cross a land like that
you own your face more: what the light
struck told a self; every rock
denied all the rest of the world

William Stafford – 'Across Kansas'

Across Texas

The left side of my face
slightly browner than the right,
the dry of El Paso's elevation
ridding the car of its mildew
and filling it with the warring scents
of West Texas desert: dust & oil.
In the mirror I wonder why I don't mind
the lines spreading out from my eyes
and widening plains of my forehead,
my ageing skin in a constant state of drought.
By the Davis Mountains a sudden shower
sends the grease in my hair running to the end of my nose
as lightning strikes the only ridge
and I give up looking for shade.
In the cheap motel of Fort Davis
I eat only popcorn for dinner.
My lips crack from salt.
I have had thousands of days
with this body clinging to me
across continents, my face
always ravenous in the rear-view
for more.

Virginia Train Song

To find the open cut you drive
looking on empty ridges for tree lines.
The coal-heart of this country staccato and thrumming.

At home they push the mesh through the aorta,
a puff of air blows out the blockage
like a child breathing away a dandelion,

the mesh settling into the myth
of train lines, that everything will pass regularly
without fanfare, only the slow chug

of things moving into place. You can't see it
but if you place your ear to the dirty chest
the throb is there. The ravage hidden

under a row of stitches tickling the nose
like the scent of downed pine trees.

A Roadrunner

Ugly bird, head too big,
running on a diagonal
like two chevrons meeting at a point.
Loss makes me tonally off
like a dry riverbed
stamped as though it's wet,
a hesitant dusty sound
that makes my eyes water.
New Mexico, your sky
more like a shell than any shell,
I tell you I too am ugly with movement,
here in Perth making a home
from scraps of memories, skeletons
of my loves in the nest.
What you gave me, Texas,
was true and empty.
In your land I was sound,
only a body resonating
in the wide expanse of the plains.
Nothing sung back that I could tell,
only the windmills and derricks
turning, the thing with feathers
just making it across the road.
Who knows if they mate for life?
If they can pick one cry out
like I can in my Bicton coffee store,
hearing only the gulls
and V8s of the highway

that leads home, all the way
away from your space
where I might have run
ugly and forever.

Prayer

Believe that every morning has a light in it
that air and soil are both nitrogen
and you are carbon and light is nuclear fission
and the half-life of what's out there is longer
than the half-life of what's in here and Believe
it's impossible for the sun to die without becoming
a red giant and Believe you've never seen
that shade of red and you never will but believe
it's beautiful like all the tail-lights in Texas
glowing together Believe what you've taken
you can return Believe that if you keep driving
to the east there is light curving to the earth
in particles or waves and gravity
is the only force you are accountable to
Believe there's a road to El Paso on the right
Believe the light will meet you there

Acknowledgements

Thanks first and foremost to Wendy, Georgia and the team at Fremantle Press for continuing to help me develop as a poet. Thanks to my family Colin, Rowena, Charlie, Greg, Hannah, Finn, Ray and Jill, for space, time, inspiration and love. Thanks to my University of Houston and University of Sydney people for reading and commenting on some of these poems, especially Kevin, Ange, Martha, Judy, Beth, Stephen Samuel, Omar, Mark, Natalie, Deb, and Mija. Special thanks to the Sitka Center for Art and Ecology, VCCA, the Department of Culture and the Arts (WA), the Dame Joan Sutherland Fund and, my favourite place, Varuna, for the resources necessary to complete this collection.

Poems have previously appeared in *The Australian* ('Organ Mountains', 'Virginia Sonnet'), *Australian Poetry Journal* ('At The Excalibur', 'First Blood Part Two'), *Island* ('Intimacy', 'You Are What This Show Is All About'), *Meanjin* ('Snow Day'), *Once Wild: Anthology of the 2014 Newcastle Poetry Prize* ('Border Crossing'), *Overland* ('Desert Meditation', 'Gods of My Youth'), *Poems for a Secular World* ('Prayer'), *Uneven Floor* ('Islands'), *Writ Poetry Review* ('Desert Meditation').

Islands
The first use of the term 'nissologist' as someone
who studies islands 'on their own terms' appeared in
Grant McCall's 1994 paper 'Nissology: A Proposal for
Consideration' in *The Journal of the Pacific Society*,
1996: 63–64, pp. 1–14.

The poem was inspired through the reading of *The Littoral
Zone: Australian Contexts and Their Writers*, C.A. Cranston
and Robert Zeller (eds), Amsterdam, Rodopi, 2007. In
particular, '*Down Home* is a psychological geography'
appears on p. 220 of Cranston's essay 'Islands' and the idea
of moons binding islands in two ways appears on p. 225.

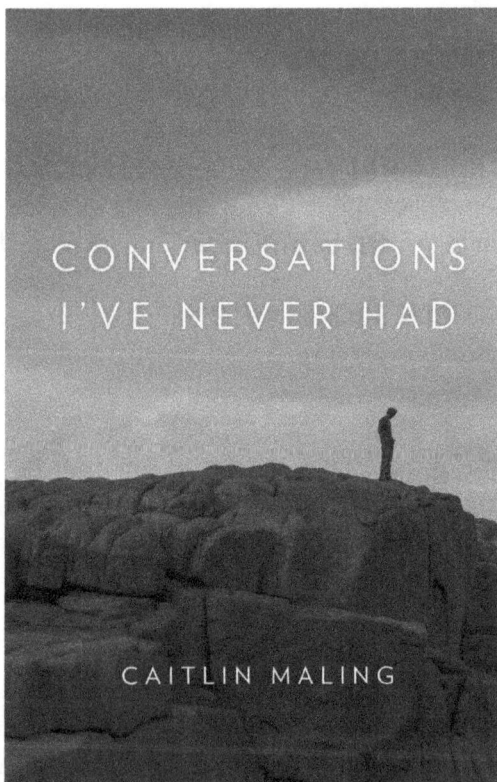

CONVERSATIONS
I'VE NEVER HAD

CAITLIN MALING

In her debut collection, award-winning talent Caitlin Maling
explores coming of age in contemporary Australia. Writing
from Perth, Houston and Cambridge, Maling's early years to
adulthood are told through the lens of the Australian landscape.
For young settler Australians this is a place that both defines and
undermines identity. A place that claims but can't be claimed in
return. Restlessly questioning and slipping between promise and
possibility, Maling's Australia is richly evoked in narratives of raw
power and feeling.

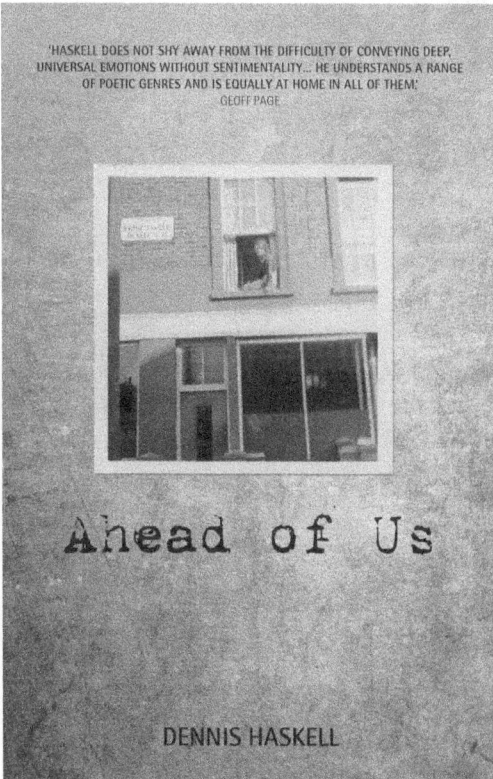

'HASKELL DOES NOT SHY AWAY FROM THE DIFFICULTY OF CONVEYING DEEP, UNIVERSAL EMOTIONS WITHOUT SENTIMENTALITY... HE UNDERSTANDS A RANGE OF POETIC GENRES AND IS EQUALLY AT HOME IN ALL OF THEM.'
GEOFF PAGE

Ahead of Us

DENNIS HASKELL

Ahead of Us is Haskell's eighth book of poetry. Dedicated to his wife Rhonda, who lost her life to cancer after a long illness, *Ahead of Us* contains poems of love, of two people forging a partnership together and of the inevitable end of that partnership when one person dies. It is a celebration of life and and of the fragile thread that holds us here.

All author royalties from the sale of this book will be donated to Cancer Council WA.

First published 2017 by
FREMANTLE PRESS
25 Quarry Street, Fremantle WA 6160
(PO Box 158, North Fremantle WA 6159)
www.fremantlepress.com.au

Consultant editor Wendy Jenkins
Cover design Carolyn Brown, www.tendeersigh.com.au
Cover photograph Ryan McGuire / Gratisography.com
Printed by Lightning Source Australia

National Library of Australia
Cataloguing-in-Publication entry

Maling, Caitlin, author.
Border crossing / Caitlin Maling.
ISBN: 9781925164367 (paperback)
Australian poetry.
Dewey Number: A821.4

Government of **Western Australia**
Department of **Culture and the Arts**

lotterywest
supported

Fremantle Press is supported by the State Government through the
Department of Culture and the Arts.

Australian Government

Australia
Council
for the Arts

Publication of this title was assisted by the Commonwealth
Government through the Australia Council, its arts funding and
advisory body.

www.ingramcontent.com/pod-product-compliance
Lightning Source LLC
Chambersburg PA
CBHW021150090426
42740CB00008B/1029